LIVING
GOD'S TRUTH
FIND PEACE IN HIS WORD.

Every page is an independent contemplation and may be read in any chosen comfortable order.

Each page begins with a reflection by the author. Verses from the King James Version of the Bible which agree with her statement, serve as a conclusion to the meditation on the page.

M. C. ABUSHAR
AUTHOR AND COVER ILLUSTRATOR

Published by MCA KIND BOOKS PRESS LLC.

Logo design by Afifeh Abou Chaar.

Copyright © 2019 by M. C. Abushar.

All rights reserved. No part of this publication may be reproduced, distributed, or transmitted in any form or by any means, including photocopying, recording, or other electronic or mechanical methods, without the prior written permission of the author, except in the case of brief quotations embodied in critical reviews and certain other noncommercial uses permitted by copyright law.

ISBN	Hardcover	978-1-7332598-5-9
	Paperback	978-1-7332598-6-6
	eBook	978-1-7332598-7-3
	Audio Book	978-1-7332598-8-0

To

JESUS CHRIST,

with gratitude and praise.

Our Lord and Saviour,
who never broke a bruised reed,
and who suffered and died
to heal the wounded.

When you're alone,
you are not alone.
When you're alone, your
inner self is free and liberated
to be united with the creator,
the God in control of all.
You are in touch with
your innermost self,
where God's Kingdom exists.

"The kingdom of God is within you."
Luke 17:21, KJV

*"And he withdrew himself into the
wilderness and prayed."*
Luke 5:16, KJV

*"Be still,
and know that I am God."*
Psalms 46:10, KJV

What you truly possess
is what you've given away. Fulfillment
in giving is greater than that resulting
from holding on
to your possessions.

*"Give to every man that asketh of thee;
and of him that taketh away thy goods
ask them not again."*
Luke 6:30, KJV

*"Give, and it shall be given unto you;
good measure, pressed down,
and shaken together,
and running over...."*
Luke 6:38, KJV

The last straw did not
break the camel's back.
It really got the camel going.
It made it leave its comfort zone
and forge ahead towards its goal
to attain success in the end.
The last straw might fracture
our outer reserve,
but it will lead our inner self
to be poured out in full force.

*"For which cause we faint not;
but though our outward man perish,
yet the inward man is renewed day by day."
2nd Corinthians 4:16, KJV*

When life humbles you,
it's preparing you
to be raised up.
The more you have
been put down,
the higher you can rise
above it all.

*"And, behold, there are last
which shall be first;
and there are first
which shall be last."
Luke 13:30, KJV*

The more you take dishonestly,
the less you have.
If you don't have God's blessing
as you acquire your possessions,
they will be fruitless to you.

*"Let him that stole steal no more:
But rather let him labour, working with
his hands the thing which is good,
that he may have to give
to him that needeth."
Ephesians 4:28, KJV*

It is advised to be grateful
and to give thanks
for the good things you have.
This is true, but it is not enough.
Give thanks not only for the good,
but for what you consider as bad,
such as loss, suffering, or grief.
Give thanks for everything.
It will become good for you.

*"In every thing give thanks:
For this is the will of God
in Christ Jesus concerning you."
1ˢᵗ Thessalonians 5:18, KJV*

*"And we know that all things
work together for good
to them that love God,
to them who are the called
according to his purpose."
Romans 8:28, KJV*

Possessions you own
with flaws in them
bring more blessings
than perfect ones.
It is vanity to take pride
in one's possessions.
A flaw in each one reminds us
to put our confidence
in spiritual reality,
where lasting riches exist.

"Sell that ye have and give alms;
provide yourselves bags that wax not old,
a treasure in the heavens that faileth not,
where no thief approacheth,
neither moth corrupteth.
For where your treasure is,
there will your heart be also."
Luke 12:33-34, KJV

It's when you're silent,
that you express yourself
the most.

*"For the kingdom of God is not
in word, but in power."*
1ˢᵗ Corinthians 4:20, KJV

Although you might be
physically blind,
you can still see true reality.
Blind people are less likely to be
distracted by the physical world
from discerning the existence
of the eternal spiritual world.

*"While we look not
at the things which are seen,
but at the things which are not seen:
For the things which are seen
are temporal;
but the things which are not seen
are eternal."
2nd Corinthians 4:18, KJV*

It's after you have worked
the hardest for God,
that you can find true rest.

*"Come unto me, all ye that labour and
are heavy laden, and I will give you rest.
Take my yoke upon you and learn of me;
for I am meek and lowly in heart:
And ye shall find rest unto your souls.
For my yoke is easy,
and my burden is light."
Matthew 11:28-30, KJV*

In our greatest pain,
our tears might be invisible.

*"Even in laughter
the heart is sorrowful."*
Proverbs 14:13, KJV

The more you feel the suffering of
others, the lighter the weight
of your hurts will become.
Look at everyone around you.
You will see a cross for each one.
The crosses differ in size,
weight, and shape, but
they are crosses, nevertheless,
and painful to carry and move on.

*"Verily I say unto you,
inasmuch as ye have done it
unto one of the least of these my
brethren, ye have done it unto me."
Matthew 25:40, KJV*

*"And our hope of you is steadfast,
knowing that as ye are
partakers of the sufferings,
so shall ye be also of the consolation."
2nd Corinthians 1:7, KJV*

Kneeling before God with
humility is not humiliation,
but liberation and protection.
It enables you to grow stronger by
letting the Holy Spirit lead you.
The Lord rewards the humble.

*His mercy is from age to age
to those who fear him.
He has shown his mighty arm and
scattered the proud in their deceit.
He has cast down the rulers
from their thrones
but lifted up the lowly.
Luke 1:50-53, KJV*

*"Wherefore take unto you
the whole armor of God, that
ye may be able to withstand in
the evil day, and having done all,
to stand. Stand therefore, having your
loins girt about with truth, and having
on the breastplate of righteousness:"
Ephesians 6:13-14, KJV*

If you like what you have today,
don't fear losing it tomorrow.
Its memory will remain with you
and continue to enrich you.
The best way to be strengthened
by treasured memories of the past
is to keep looking forward
without looking back.

*And Jesus said unto him,
"No man, having put his hand
to the plow, and looking back,
is fit for the kingdom of God."
Luke 9:62, KJV*

Do not depend on others
for your needs.
Turn to God as your source,
and your inner strength
will grow to sustain you.

*"Thus saith the Lord;
Cursed be the man that
trusteth in man."
Jeremiah 17:5, KJV*

*"Blessed is the man that
trusteth in the Lord,
and whose hope
the Lord is."
Jeremiah 17:7, KJV*

*"Finally, my brethren,
be strong in the Lord and
in the power of his might."
Ephesians 6:10, KJV*

What brings enrichment
to one's life
is not the quantity
of one's possessions,
but the number of virtues
that God wills us to possess.

*"Love not the world, neither
the things that are in the world.
If any man love the world,
the love of the Father is not in him.
And the world passeth away,
and the lust thereof:
But he that doeth the will of God
abideth forever."
1st John 2:15, 17, KJV*

You might think you need
to be loved to be happy.
The truth is that you
need to love
to feel content.

*"For this is the message that
ye heard from the beginning,
that we should love one another."
1st John 3:11, KJV*

*"God is love; and he that dwelleth in love
dwelleth in God,
and God in him."
1st John 4:16, KJV*

You might think that
your life will be right when
you get rid of a cross you have.
The truth is that your life will be right
when you accept your cross.

*"And he said to them all,
if any man will come after me,
let him deny himself,
and take up his cross daily,
and follow me.
For whosoever will save his life
shall lose it: but whosoever
will lose his life for my sake,
the same shall save it."*
Luke 9:23-24, KJV

When we are injured,
we find inner joy.
You will always discover
some felicity accompanying
the wound in your heart.

*"They that sow in tears
shall reap in joy."
Psalm 126:5, KJV*

*"And ye shall be sorrowful,
but your sorrow
shall be turned into joy."
John 16:20, KJV*

Often, when we feel
that it's time to rest,
we must work even harder.

*"But wrought with labour and travail
night and day, that we might not
be chargeable to any of you:
Not because we have not power,
but to make ourselves an example
unto you to follow us."
2nd Thessalonians 3:8-9, KJV*

If you wish to lead others
in carrying their crosses,
you must demonstrate by
carrying the heavier cross.

*"But we see Jesus, who was
made a little lower than the angels
for the suffering of death,
crowned with glory and honour;
that he by the grace of God
should taste death for every man."
Hebrews 2:9, KJV*

Freedom is being subjected
to the Word of God.

*Then said Jesus to those Jews
which believed on him,
"If ye continue in my word,
then are ye my disciples indeed;
and ye shall know the truth,
and the truth shall make you free."
John 8:31-32, KJV*

When you leave your comfort zone to do good deeds, you will find God in your heart.

"Go ye therefore, and teach all nations, baptizing them in the name of the Father, and of the Son, and of the Holy Ghost: Teaching them to observe all things whatsoever I have commanded you: And, lo, I am with you always, even unto the end of the world. Amen." Matthew 28:19-20, KJV

When you slow down, God
will take over and move fast
against your enemies.

*And Moses said unto the people,
"Fear ye not, stand still,
and see the salvation of the Lord,
which he will show to you today:
For the Egyptians
whom ye have seen today,
ye shall see them again
no more forever.
The Lord shall fight for you,
and ye shall hold your peace."
Exodus 14:13-14, KJV*

When you decide
to settle for less,
you will receive more.
Contentment with
what you have
is pleasing to God.
He will send you
more as a reward.

*"But godliness with contentment
is great gain.
For we brought nothing into this world,
and it is certain we can carry nothing out.
And having food and raiment,
let us be therewith content."
1st Timothy 6:6-8, KJV*

It's the one who is serving
others, who is the true leader.
If you're willing to listen
when another has a problem,
and if you're there to lend
a helping hand when
a job needs to be done,
then you're the greater one.

*"But he that is greatest among you
shall be your servant.
And whosoever shall exalt himself
shall be abased;
and he that shall humble
himself shall be exalted."
Matthew 23:11-12, KJV*

Discover who you really are
by not choosing a personality
for yourself. God has already
defined a character for you.
Find it and live it to the fullest.

*"Before I formed thee in the belly I knew
thee; and before thou camest forth out of
the womb I sanctified thee, and I ordained
thee a prophet unto the nations."*
Jeremiah 1:5, KJV

God might choose to
bring you close to an evil doer.
It might be His Will for you
to serve the person who is
committing evil deeds against you.
Give thanks for God's Holy Will,
and obey Him by serving the
person you think you should avoid.

*"But I say unto you which hear:
Love your enemies,
do good to them which hate you,
bless them that curse you, and pray
for them which despitefully use you."
Luke 6:27-28, KJV*

When you do good to others,
it doesn't ensure that they
will be led to Christ. But it
will certainly perfect you
and bless you with the
Lord's favour on you.

*"Now the God of Peace, that brought
again from the dead our Lord Jesus,
that great Shepherd of the sheep, through
the blood of the everlasting covenant,
make you perfect in every good work
to do His Will, working in you that
which is well-pleasing in his sight
through Jesus Christ; to whom
be glory forever and ever. Amen."
Hebrews 13:20-21, KJV*

*"Do good, and lend, hoping for nothing
again; and your reward shall be great, and
ye shall be the children of the Highest."
Luke 6:35, KJV*

There is no detail in our life
that is too insignificant for God.
We might exclude Him from
everyday routine activities,
but He will still intervene
and use them to fulfill
His Will in our lives.

"Are not five sparrows sold for two farthings, and not one of them is forgotten before God? But even the very hairs of your head are all numbered. Fear not therefore: Ye are of more value than many sparrows."
Luke 12:6-7, KJV

You might wish to get rid
of your troubles to find peace.
However, the Lord wills you to
have peace amidst your problems.
We cannot understand this, but
we know that we have been
promised the peace that
passes all understanding.

*"Be careful for nothing; but in
every thing by prayer and supplication
with thanksgiving let your requests be
known unto God. And the peace of God,
which passeth all understanding,
shall keep your hearts and minds
through Christ Jesus."
Philippians 4:6-7, KJV*

You might think that you need the happiness that comes by winning a prize, money, or a vacation to relieve you from your grief. The truth is that your sorrow might be granting you more spiritual good than any material thing you might win. God sends us what is in our best interest at every step of our life's journey.

"For our light affliction, which is but for a moment, worketh for us a far more exceeding and eternal weight of glory."
2nd Corinthians 4:17, KJV

"But the God of all grace, who hath called called us unto his eternal glory by Christ Jesus, after that ye have suffered a while, make you perfect, stablish, strengthen, settle you."
1st Peter 5:10, KJV

You might prefer not to do a job because you believe that you cannot do it well. But God might intend for you to do it while relying on Him to lead you, rather than to depend on yourself. He might will for you to surrender to Him and let Him guide you. He will empower you with strength and wisdom to accomplish the task His way and be pleasing to Him.

"But Jesus beheld them, and said unto them: With men this is impossible; but with God, all things are possible."
Matthew 19:26, KJV

"I am crucified with Christ: Nevertheless, I live; yet not I, but Christ liveth in me."
Galatians 2:20, KJV

"I can do all things through Christ which strengtheneth me."
Philippians 4:13, KJV

When you worry about a problem that might arise in the future, you are not concentrating on the evil that is threatening you right now. God helps us to overcome attacks by the devil when our attention is focused on Him and the issue facing us at that specific moment. Don't add to the problems of today by taking on those for tomorrow. Each day brings enough evil.

*"Take therefore no thought
for the morrow;
for the morrow shall take
thought for the things of itself.
Sufficient unto the day
is the evil thereof."
Matthew 6:34, KJV*

As a child of God,
don't expect to be rewarded
by others for the good you do.
You might end up losing
your reward from God.

"Take heed that ye do not your alms before men, to be seen of them: Otherwise ye have no reward of your Father, which is in heaven. Therefore, when thou doest thine alms, do not sound a trumpet before thee, as the hypocrites do in the synagogues and in the streets, that they may have glory of men. Verily I say unto you, they have their reward. But when thou doest alms, let not thy left hand know what thy right hand doeth: That thine alms may be in secret: And thy Father, which seeth in secret himself shall reward thee openly."
Matthew 6:1-4, KJV

The only way to resist evil
is to surrender to God.
Only then will we have the
ability to overcome the enemy.
Humans are no match for the devil.
Allowing the Holy Spirit to lead us
is the only weapon we possess to
deflect Satan's poison back to him.
It is a powerful sword that's stronger
than any weapon used against us.

*"Submit yourselves therefore to God.
Resist the devil, and he will flee from you."
James 4:7, KJV*

*"And take the helmet of salvation,
and the sword of the Spirit,
which is the Word of God."
Ephesians 6:17, KJV*

The greatness of leaders is not based on the degree to which they are loved by their followers, but rather on the amount of love that they have for their followers. Jesus, our Lord, loved us more than any person would love us.

"Greater love hath no man than this, that a man lay down his life for his friends."
John 15:13, KJV

When you sincerely care for others, you are there for them even when they are not seeking help for themselves.

"Now we exhort you, brethren, warn them that are unruly, comfort the feeble-minded, support the weak, be patient toward all men. See that none render evil for evil unto any man; but ever follow that which is good, both among yourselves, and to all men."
1st Thessalonians 5:14-15, KJV

You must never fear anyone other than God. Don't fear those who can only harm the body. God can send a soul to hell after He kills an enemy of His people. Fear of God casts away fear of everything else.

"And I say unto you my friends, be not afraid of them that kill the body, and after that have no more that they can do. But I will forewarn you whom ye shall fear: Fear Him, which after He hath killed, hath power to cast into hell; yea, I say unto you, fear Him."
Luke 12:4-5, KJV

"For God hath not given us the spirit of fear; but of power, and of love, and of a sound mind."
2nd Timothy 1:7, KJV

When you knock at a door
and it doesn't open,
don't assume that you are
not meant to enter.
It might be that you shouldn't
go through it now, but that at
some future time, you may be
allowed to cross its threshold.

*"To every thing there is a season,
and a time to every purpose
under the heaven."
Ecclesiastes 3:1, KJV*

You might be proud of your
possessions or achievements.
The truth is that you should only
be proud of God's mercy and grace,
which you received thanks to
Christ's dying on the cross.

*"But God forbid that I should glory, save
in the cross of our Lord Jesus Christ."
Galatians 6:14, KJV*

*"For by grace are ye saved through faith;
and that not of yourselves:
It is the gift of God: Not of works,
lest any man should boast.
For we are His workmanship,
created in Christ Jesus unto good works,
which God hath before ordained
that we should walk in them."
Ephesians 2:8-10, KJV*

You might be searching for a person to reciprocate your love. Although we cannot guarantee that another human will love us in return, we know that when we love Jesus, God will love us and be closer to us than anyone else.

"For the Father himself loveth you, because ye have loved me, and have believed that I came out from God."
John 16:27, KJV

"And there is a friend that sticketh closer than a brother."
Proverbs, 18:24, KJV

When you develop true
wisdom in the Lord,
you will not only accept the
crosses you already have,
but will choose additional ones.
This is true because you will
realize how precious it is for your
soul to follow in the steps of Jesus.
You will be willing to give up
everything to enter His Kingdom.

*"Confirming the souls of the disciples, and
exhorting them to continue in the faith,
and that we must through much tribulation
enter the kingdom of God."
Acts 14:22, KJV*

*"And he that taketh not his cross, and
followeth after me, is not worthy of me.
He that findeth his life shall lose it:
And he that loseth his life
for my sake shall find it."
Matthew 10:38-39, KJV*

You cannot love one person
and hate another. You will
either love both or hate both.
When you love, you are serving God.
When you hate, you are
serving the devil.

"No man can serve two masters.
Ye cannot serve God and mammon."
Matthew 6:24, KJV

When someone disappoints you,
it will be good for your soul.
You will trust and love Jesus
more than anyone else.

*"He that loveth father or mother more
than me is not worthy of me: And he that
loveth son or daughter more than me
is not worthy of me."
Matthew 10:37, KJV*

It is harder to live for Christ
than to die for Christ.
It takes more courage to choose
to continue serving others than
to decide to die and be with Christ.
The pain and hardship endured while
overcoming the evil in this world are
more difficult than taking on death.
Nevertheless, the reward will be
eternal light and rest in heaven.

*"For I am in a strait betwixt two,
having a desire to depart,
and to be with Christ;
which is far better:
nevertheless, to abide in the flesh
is more needful for you."
Philippians 1:23-24, KJV*

*Then shall the righteous
shine forth as the sun
in the kingdom of their Father.
Matthew 13:43, KJV*

If you are sad because you think
that God has grown distant and left
you to bear your burdens alone,
be reassured that He never moved
away from you. It was you who
let go of His guiding hand.
You must seek God first
before reaching out to another,
and God will draw closer to you.

*"Draw nigh to God,
and he will draw nigh to you...."
James 4:8, KJV*

*"And Jesus answered him:
The first of all the commandments is:
Hear, O Israel:
The Lord our God is one Lord:
and thou shalt love the Lord thy God
with all thy heart, and with all thy soul,
and with all thy mind,
and with all thy strength:
this is the first commandment."
Mark 12:29-30, KJV*

God didn't command you not
to seek revenge because your
enemy shouldn't be punished.
It was to protect you from
reciprocating the harm committed
against you and be found guilty.
On the contrary, God will inflict a
greater punishment on your enemies
than you ever can. He prepared their
reward in hell, where their screaming
will never stop in fires that never end.

*Never take revenge my dear friends.
It is written: "It is mine to take revenge;
I will pay them back," says the Lord.
Romans 12:19, KJV*

*The Son of man shall send forth
his angels, and they shall gather out of
his kingdom all things that offend,
and shall cast them into a furnace
of fire; there shall be wailing
and gnashing of teeth.
Matthew 13:41-42*

If you don't possess the love of Christ, no logic or argument you give to preach Him will express His Truth.

"Though I speak with the tongues of men and of angels, and have not charity, I am become as sounding brass, or a tinkling cymbal."
1st Corinthians 13:1, KJV

Don't hesitate to bless others
for fear that it might hurt you
and distance you from God.
The truth is that if they are not
worthy of your blessing,
it will return to you,
and you will be blessed
with the peace of God.

*"And when ye come into a house, salute it.
And if the house be worthy,
let your peace come upon it:
But if it be not worthy,
let your peace return to you."
Matthew 10:12-13, KJV*

If you're patient most of the time
with demands made on you by
people around you, but become
impatient with one person, you
still do not possess God's love.
You will become patient with
everyone all the time,
when the love of God
fills your heart completely.

*"Charity suffereth long and is kind.
[Charity] beareth all things,
and endureth all things.
Charity never faileth."
1st Corinthians 13:4, 7, 8, KJV*

You might assume that someone
who has a lot of worldly possessions,
has all that one would wish to own.
The truth is that only the person
who dwells in the Kingdom of God
with the Holy Spirit, possesses
the most precious belonging.

*"And I will pray to the Father, and he shall
give you another Comforter, that he may
live in you forever. Even the Spirit of truth,
whom the world cannot receive because it
neither sees him nor knows him. But ye
know him; for he dwelleth with you."
John 14:16-17, KJV*

*"Again, the Kingdom of Heaven is like
unto a merchantman, seeking goodly
pearls: Who, when he had found
one pearl of great price,
went and sold all that he had,
and bought it."
Matthew 13:45, KJV*

About the Author

M. C. Abushar is an educator, author, artist, and pianist. As educator, she specialized in providing children with academic excellence, inspiration for spiritual growth, motivation to participate in moral decision-making, and opportunities to serve others. Her experience as principal of a parochial school in Los Angeles, granted her mastery of conversing with pupils in the primary grades. During the four years of her attendance at doctoral classes while simultaneously serving as full-time principal, she published Living God's Truth, find Peace in His Word. It received the Mom's Choice Award® honouring excellence and a five-star review rating by OnlineBookClub.org.

As author and artist, M. C. Abushar left her position as principal to create picture books. URL https://www.amazon.com/dp/B0CTHRNSK8.

The Tyler the Rabbit tales model the truth said by Jesus Christ, in a style that inspires the child to copy and practice the precept presented. "It is more blessed to give than to receive." Acts 20:35 KJV.

As pianist, M. C. Abushar posted on YouTube her performance of "Le Lac de Côme" by French composer Giselle Galos, who aimed the piece to evoke the calm and serenity that a visitor gains while viewing Lake Como in Italy. URL https://YouTu.be/rAqqy3ztCMk.

www.ingramcontent.com/pod-product-compliance
Lightning Source LLC
Chambersburg PA
CBHW061225070526
44584CB00029B/3993